A Chum for Tot

By Sally Cowan

Tot walks out of the den.

A quick moth whips by Tot!

But the moth did not want to chat with Tot.

It flaps its long wings to dash away.

Mon sat on a thick log.

Mon is in a rush to get nuts for his mum.

A gull and its chick dash off when Tot walks up to them.

Then Tot got a whiff of fish!

I am Tot!
I am Chad!
This is such a big fish!
Do you want a bit?

Yum! Shall we be chums?
Yes!

CHECKING FOR MEANING

1. What does Tot wish she had? *(Literal)*
2. Why can't Mon chat with Tot? *(Literal)*
3. Why did the gull and its chick run from Tot? *(Inferential)*

EXTENDING VOCABULARY

moth	What does a moth look like? What other creature is similar to a moth? What parts of a moth do you know?
chat	Say all the sounds in the word *chat*. What word would you make if you replaced the *ch* with *c*?
whiff	What happened when *Tot got a whiff of fish*? What word could the author have used instead of *whiff*?

MOVING BEYOND THE TEXT

1. Where might you meet a new friend? How would you introduce yourself to a new friend?
2. What does it mean to be a good friend?
3. Which animal in the story is your favourite? Why?
4. What do you think happens to Tot after the end of the story?

SPEED SOUNDS

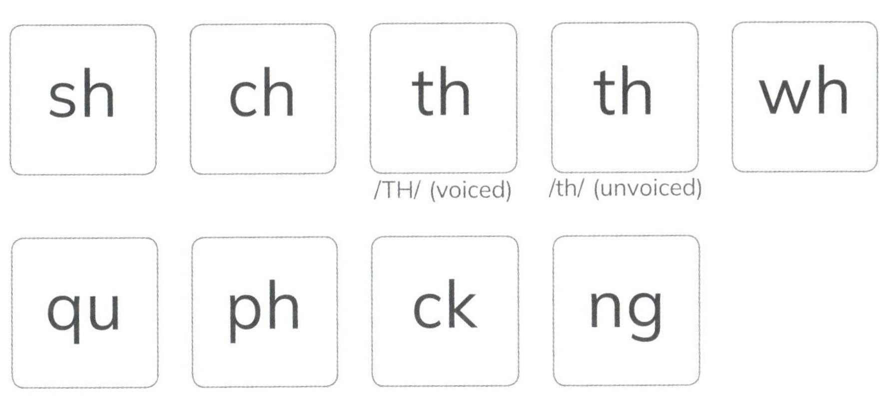

PRACTICE WORDS